Six
CHOICES THAT
WILL CHANGE
YOUR LIFE

Six
CHOICES THAT WILL CHANGE YOUR LIFE

Carol Kent & Karen Lee-Thorp

NAVPRESS®

BRINGING TRUTH TO LIFE

OUR GUARANTEE TO YOU

We believe so strongly in the message of our books that we are making this quality guarantee to you. If for any reason you are disappointed with the content of this book, return the title page to us with your name and address and we will refund to you the list price of the book. To help us serve you better, please briefly describe why you were disappointed. Mail your refund request to: NavPress, P.O. Box 35002, Colorado Springs, CO 80935.

The Navigators is an international Christian organization. Our mission is to advance the gospel of Jesus and His kingdom into the nations through spiritual generations of laborers living and discipling among the lost. We see a vital movement of the gospel, fueled by prevailing prayer, flowing freely through relational networks and out into the nations where workers for the kingdom are next door to everywhere.

NavPress is the publishing ministry of The Navigators. The mission of NavPress is to reach, disciple, and equip people to know Christ and make Him known by publishing life-related materials that are biblically rooted and culturally relevant. Our vision is to stimulate spiritual transformation through every product we publish.

NAVPRESS, BRINGING TRUTH TO LIFE, and the NAVPRESS logo are registered trademarks of NavPress. Absence of ® in connection with marks of NavPress or other parties does not indicate an absence of registration of those marks.

ISBN 1-57683-206-6

Cover photo by Gary Buss/FPG International
Cover design by Jennifer Mahalik
Creative Team: Amy Spencer, Terry Behimer, Tim Howard, Heather Nordyke, Pat Miller

Some of the anecdotal illustrations in this book are true to life and are included with the permission of the persons involved. All other illustrations are composites of real situations, and any resemblance to people living or dead is coincidental.

Unless otherwise identified, all Scripture quotations in this publication are taken from the *HOLY BIBLE: NEW INTERNATIONAL VERSION* ® (NIV®). Copyright © 1973, 1978, 1984 by International Bible Society. Used by permission of Zondervan Publishing House. All rights reserved. Other version used: *The Message: New Testament with Psalms and Proverbs* (MSG) by Eugene H. Peterson, copyright © 1993, 1994, 1995, used by permission of NavPress Publishing Group.

Printed in the United States of America

4 5 6 7 8 9 10 11 12 13 14 15 16 17 / 11 10 09 08 07 06

FOR A FREE CATALOG OF
NAVPRESS BOOKS & BIBLE STUDIES,
CALL 1-800-366-7788 (USA)
OR 1-800-839-4769 (CANADA)

CONTENTS

INTRODUCTION

Choices Matter

THERE'S a popular poster that reads: "If you don't know where you're going, you'll probably wind up somewhere else." That's how many people live: consumed with today's urgency, unaware of what a difference an important choice could make. So much of life seems to happen to us, and we are swept downstream in the flood. So many things are out of our control. When life is pouring down in buckets, it's easy to feel helpless.

But we're not helpless. Many things are out of our control, yet every day brings opportunities for us to make choices that really count, decisions that set the course not only of our lives but also of the lives we influence. In the large scheme of things, these choices are vastly more important than what long-distance phone company we'll use or what car we'll drive.

Jesus is our model of One who made the important choices carefully and wisely. By observing *what* He chose and *how* He went about it, we can begin to notice how many powerful choices life offers us. And we can begin to make those choices consciously and well. In this study we'll look at six choices Jesus made consistently. He didn't control the interruptions in His day, but He chose how to respond to them. He chose to obey God rather than control His world. He chose compassion over convenience and forgiveness over anger. He didn't run from suffering but chose His response to it. And He chose to use His hard-earned wisdom to cast vision for those who would outlive Him. We aren't the Son of God, but we have the power to make every one of those choices, and more.

We're not in control of our worlds, and we don't have to be. God is. But we're not helpless either. When we choose to stop trying to control, we find we can choose to use the abilities we *do* have. When we make decisions based on Christ's example and biblical principles instead of mere emotions, we build confidence, hope, and courage, and we take positive action.

Do you know where you're going? Would you like to live less by accident and more "on purpose"? We think you can—but don't take our word for it. Come and see what Jesus has to say.

How to Use This Guide

You were born to be a woman of influence. No—we don't mean a busybody or a queen bee, telling others what to do or making their lives revolve around yours. You were born to model your life on Jesus' life, and in so doing, be a model for others. Perhaps your influence will happen in a few quiet words over coffee, in a hug or a prayer. Don't say, "Not me—I'm barely treading water!" If you have the Spirit of God in your life, you have what it takes. God wants to influence people through you.

We've created these *Designed for Influence* Bible studies to draw out this loving, serving, celebrating side of you. You can use this study guide in your private time with God, but you'll gain even more from it if you meet with a small group of other women who share your desire to grow and give. The study is designed around the seven life-changing principles explored in Carol Kent's book, *Becoming a Woman of Influence*. These principles, which underlay Jesus' style of influencing others, are:

- Time alone with God
- Walking and talking
- Storytelling
- Asking questions
- Compassion
- Unconditional love
- Casting vision

Each of the six sessions in this guide contains these seven sections:

An Opening Story. When you see the word "I" in this guide, you're hearing from Carol. She begins each session with a story from her own life to let you know we're not making this stuff up in some spiritual hothouse; we care about these issues because we're living them. As you read these stories, look for a point of connection between your life and Carol's.

Connecting. Next comes your chance to tell your own story about the topic at hand. If you're studying on your own, take a few minutes to write down a piece of your life story in response to the questions in this section. If you're meeting with a group, tell your stories to each other. Nothing brings a group of women together like sharing stories. It's not necessary for each person to answer every question in the rest of the study, but each person should have a chance to respond to the "Connecting" questions. Sharing stories is great fun, but try to keep your answers brief so that you'll have time for the rest of the study!

Learning from the Master. The entire Bible is the Word of God. Yet Jesus Himself is the Word of God made flesh. The Bible studies in this series focus on Jesus' words and actions in the Gospels. You'll get to see how Jesus Himself grappled with situations much like those you face. He's the smartest guy in history, the closest to the Father, the one who understood life better than anyone else. This is your opportunity to follow Him around and watch how He did it. If you're meeting with a group, you don't need to answer the questions ahead of time, but it would be helpful to read through them and begin thinking about them. When your group gathers, ask for one or more volunteers to read the Scripture aloud. If the story is lengthy, you could take turns reading paragraphs. Or if you really want to have fun, assign the roles of Jesus and the other characters to different readers. Karen wrote the Bible study section of this guide, and if you have any questions or comments, you can e-mail her at bible.study@navpress.com.

A Reflection. This section contains some thoughts on the topic as well as some questions that invite you to apply what you've learned to your own life. If you're meeting with a group, it is helpful, but not necessary, to read the reflection ahead of time. When your group reaches this point in the study, you can allow people a few minutes to read over the reflection to refresh their memories. Talk about the ideas in this section that seem especially helpful to you.

Talking with God. This section closes your meeting if you're studying with a group. Inviting God to enable you to live what you've discussed may be the most important thing you do together. In addition to the prayer ideas suggested in this section, feel free to include your personal concerns.

Time Alone with God. This section and the next are your "homework" if you are meeting with a group. The first part of your "homework" is to take some time during the week to be with God. In this section you'll find ideas for prayer, journaling, thinking, or just *being* with God. If you're already accustomed to taking time away from the rush of life to reflect and pray, then you know how these quiet moments energize you for the rest of your week. If you've believed yourself to be "too busy" to take this time to nourish your hungry soul, then this is your chance to taste the feast God has prepared for you.

Walking with Others. The second part of your "homework" is to pass on God's love to someone else in some way. Here you'll sample what it means to be a woman of influence simply by giving away something you've received. This is your chance to practice compassion, unconditional love, and vision-casting with the women you encounter in your daily life.

That's how the Christian life works: we draw apart to be with God, then we go back into the world to love as we have been loved.

If you're meeting with a group, one woman will need to take responsibility for facilitating the discussion at each meeting. You can rotate this responsibility or let the same person facilitate all six sessions. The facilitator's main task is to keep the discussion moving forward and to make sure everyone has a chance to speak. This will be easiest if you limit the size of your discussion group to no more than eight people. If your group is larger than eight (especially in a Sunday school class), consider dividing into subgroups of four to six people for your discussion.

Spiritual influence is not just for super-Christians. You can make a difference in someone's life by letting God work through you. Take a chance—the results may surprise you!

1

USE INTERRUPTIONS AS GOD - APPOINTMENTS

You go nowhere by accident.

—DR. RICHARD HALVERSON [1]

ELIZABETH caught my eye, waved, and called across the parking lot, "Do you have time for a cup of coffee?"

I groaned. That day I didn't have time for *any* extra appointments. I had to go to the bank, stop by the cleaners, pick up a prescription, and attend a leaders' meeting for Bible study. My house was a mess after entertaining weekend company. I was feeling stressed and agitated.

But there was something in Elizabeth's eyes and voice that made me pause. Out of my mouth came these words: "Having coffee is a great idea. I haven't caught up with what's happening in your life in a long time. Where shall we meet?"

A few minutes later we sat across from each other in a little café in a nearby mall. As soon as our coffee was ordered I could see tears in her eyes. "Rob and I are having a rough time right now. He told me he doesn't love me anymore and he really doesn't know if he *ever* loved me. Both of the kids know something is wrong. Angela came into the kitchen while I was cleaning up after dinner last night. She was crying and said, 'Are you and Daddy getting a divorce?' I didn't know what to tell her. I haven't talked to anybody about this because I feel so miserable, but when I saw you in the school parking lot this morning, I knew you would understand and that you would give me a listening ear and some helpful advice. I don't know what to do or where to turn."

There was nothing I could say or do that day to make Elizabeth's pain go away, but I wept with her and embraced her grief. Together we made a list of steps she could take to encourage Rob to consider marriage counseling before they took more drastic action. I recommended a pastor she could call. After she shared more details about the situation, I told her I had a book I'd be dropping off at her house later in the day that addressed some of the issues she was dealing with. I spoke openly of a time in my own marriage when I thought it would be easier to walk away from a tough problem than to face it and work on a positive solution. She looked up and said, "You and Gene have had some challenging times in your marriage, too? I always thought you two had it all together." We both laughed.

By the end of our conversation, I could see hope in her eyes. She knew there were choices and options that could produce a solution that would honor God and protect her marriage. Most of all, she knew she wasn't alone. We prayed and hugged before each of us walked back to our cars and resumed our daily routine. That day an unexpected and unwanted interruption in my day was actually a "God-appointment" in disguise. In this session we'll look at how Jesus dealt with interruptions as clues to God's agenda for His day.

1. If you're meeting with a group, take a minute or two to describe what a typical Tuesday is like for you.

In a culture that worships efficiency, time is something to be managed, spent, or saved like money. It can be hard for us to shift our focus from *productivity* to *fruitfulness*. But Jesus valued people over products. So when a person in need broke into His day's business, He treated the event not as an interruption, but as a God-appointment.

2. Read Mark 5:21-43. What was Jesus' agenda before the bleeding woman turned up?

3. When Jesus realized that power had gone out of Him (verse 30), He stopped and looked around for the person who had sought His healing. Why do you think He did this? After all, the woman was healed. Why did He delay His journey to the dying girl?

According to the customs of the day, a woman should never touch a rabbi. A bleeding person was ritually unclean and should never touch anyone. That's why the woman was so afraid when she spoke to Jesus.

4. How would you describe Jesus' attitude toward the "unclean" woman?

The synagogue ruler was an important leader in the community. The bleeding woman was nobody, more invisible than a homeless person on one of our city streets.

5. Who are the "synagogue rulers" in your life, the people whose status gives them a right to your immediate and undivided attention?

6. Who are the "bleeding women" in your world, the people who have no automatic right to interrupt you?

7. The delay didn't prevent Jesus from carrying out His original plan, even though the little girl died. That's not always true for us. Sometimes accepting an interruption means letting other things on our agenda slide. What would it cost you to treat each interruption as a God-appointment with a human being?

8. What is the value of doing that?

9. Read Mark 1:35-39. Once again, Jesus is interrupted in the middle of something important. How is His response here different from His response to the woman's interruption?

A New Perspective on Interruptions

When we see each day as an opportunity to be a representative of Jesus Christ, we take on a new mindset. As people enter our lives in unexpected ways, we often view these interruptions as unwanted and unproductive intrusions in our day. However, to the Christian, every interruption should be viewed with a different perspective:

- *See the person, not the interruption.* Look beyond the inconvenience of the moment and into the eyes and/or ears of the person who interrupts you. My friend Nan led a marketing analyst to Christ over the telephone because she first took the time to respond to survey questions she didn't really care about answering. In the process of listening, Nan realized how much this woman needed a personal faith relationship with Christ. She turned an interruption into an important appointment.

• *Recognize the value of "unplanned ministry."* As a detailed planner and agendakeeper, I have often valued getting through my to-do list more than meeting the needs of someone who interrupts my schedule. Often the most important tasks God has planned for us to participate in today were not on our written (or mental) agenda.

• *Strive for balance—knowing the difference between a God-appointment and an unnecessary interruption.* A God-appointment occurs when one person has a need—emotional, spiritual, or physical—and another person makes herself available to meet that need. This often happens unexpectedly. Ask God to give you the discernment to recognize when someone is only hungry for attention and when someone has a genuine need. Pray also to discern needs you are called to address and needs that exceed your limits. Not even Jesus tried to meet every need He saw. Also, sometimes you will be the one with a need, and God will interrupt your life with someone who can help to meet it.

• *Develop a list of questions that will help you influence others' lives in meaningful ways.* One of the kindest gifts we can give to someone who interrupts our day is to listen to her without finishing her sentences, letting her complete her thoughts while we give her good eye (or ear) contact.

While you listen, pray for the spiritual insight to ask the right questions. Some possibilities are:

- What brings you here today?
- Is there anything more I need to know about this situation?
- What can I do to help?
- How can I pray for you?

The choice to use interruptions as God-appointments will change your life by making you more spiritually fruitful and less frustrated each and every day.

> The real voyage of discovery consists not in seeking new landscapes, but in having new eyes.
>
> —MARCEL PROUST[2]

10. What appeals to you about using interruptions as God-appointments?

11. What questions or concerns do you have about doing this?

12. What, if anything, will you do differently this week as a result of exploring this subject?

Think of someone who has recently interrupted your day. It might be a delivery person, an annoyed customer, or a child. Include that person in your prayers with your group.

Reflect on the interruptions you have had in the past twenty-four hours. Write down a list of the names or jobs of the people who interrupted you: your coworker Mary, a telemarketer, your four-year-old, and so on. Ask God to show you the need in the life of each of these people. Pray for each person. When you're done, ask God to show you the need in the life of each person who interrupts you tomorrow.

> *Don't bother to give God instructions; just report for duty.*
>
> —CORRIE TEN BOOM [3]

The choice to follow Jesus always leads us into other people's lives, where Jesus is already at work. Some of us are only too eager to give others advice and meet their needs. But some of us get caught up in our own concerns, or we doubt we have anything to offer others. Yet all of us can learn to be women of influence in a spirit of humility.

Watch this week for a God-appointment with someone who needs your friendship, especially a woman who is younger or newer in faith than you. Use one or more of the questions listed on page 21 following *"Develop a list of questions . . . "* to reach out to this person.

You don't have to commit to "mentoring" her for years. Just agree with God that you're available to be present for that woman, to encourage her, to be whatever God would like you to be in her life for this season. *This season* might be a single contact with a stranger, or a friendship of a few weeks or months. It might grow into a long-term friendship. You're not on the hook forever; just agree with God to be available, and ask God what's needed.

2

CHOOSE OBEDIENCE
OVER CONTROL

*The moment we "purpose in our heart" to obey Him,
at that instant He comes to help us. His incomparable
gift is the ability to obey, to move out into what
usually looks like uncharted and dangerous country.*

—CATHERINE MARSHALL[1]

MY husband sounded jubilant: "Honey, the vice president of the company just called, and I've been invited to take a job at the home office in Fort Wayne, Indiana. It's a great business opportunity, and I know we'll love living in a larger city."

My heart dropped to my stomach. I was in the dream job of my life—directing an alternative education program for pregnant teenagers. I knew I was making a difference in the lives of young women who were going through tremendous challenges. How could my husband even *think* of leaving this cozy little town where we knew everybody and felt like an integral part of our church and our community?

As the events and decisions of the next few days unfolded, I did everything in my power to control the outcome of this situation. I created a detailed list of every reason why we should stay in our town. I also listed everything I had looked for in a job that would be perfectly suited to my gifts—and then matched up my gifts with a column on the opposite side of the paper that demonstrated how well this job met those criteria. Those lists were all about what *I* had done and the importance of getting *my way* in this important decision.

As we were preparing for bed one night, Gene calmly said, "Carol, how would you feel about praying together for several days about this job offer before I get back to the home office with a response?" I piously said it was a great idea, knowing ahead of time that God would most certainly reveal to my husband that we should stay right where we were!

Once we'd started praying together about the possible move, I found myself praying about it on my own. And one day, to my complete surprise, God spoke to me—not in an audible way, but in that deep "inner knowing" kind of way—and I realized that this job opportunity was a dream my husband had had for a long time. It was as important to him as my current position was to me! Then, as I continued to struggle privately with the thought that I was trying to control the situation instead of responding to God's direction, I went to my weekly Bible study. The entire lesson was on obedience, and in summary that day my instructor asked, "What act of obedience does Jesus ask of you so that the situation might be transformed? What do you envision Jesus doing as you cooperate with Him?"

Within a short time, God confirmed to both Gene and me that this was a move He was going to use in *both* of our lives. When I gave up my control of the situation and said yes to the possibility of moving, my apprehension turned into expectation. This move turned out to be the best decision we could have made — for our spiritual growth as well as for both of our careers. What I would have missed if I had hung onto my control, instead of obediently following God's direction for our future! In this session we'll discover the practical benefits of doing things Jesus' way.

1. What is one thing in your life that you really like to have done *your* way? (It might be something as simple as coffee.)

The Greek word *Christos* (Christ) means "the Anointed One." Among Jews of Jesus' day, it signified "the King," the person anointed to be king of God's kingdom. Kings have gone out of fashion in our time; in most Western countries, we believe in democracy. But the kingdom of God is a realm in which each of us, from the smallest child to the most influential Christian leader, reports directly to the top. Jesus has the right to give us orders and expects us to carry them out.

In this day, when all authority is viewed with suspicion and cynicism, the idea of taking orders bothers many of us. Does taking orders mean we are robots, not allowed to think or choose for ourselves? Does Jesus have our best interests at heart? Or is He like the dad who rules his children arbitrarily and selfishly, or the boss who wants to squeeze as much work out of his employees as possible, or the politician who will say and do anything to stay in office?

One of the bedrock choices we make every day is either to obey the quiet voice of God or to try to control our lives. God will not send us to hell for disobeying Him; the blood of Jesus covers all the disobedience of those who believe in Him. But the question remains: if we believe in Him, why on earth do we hesitate to obey Him? This is the question Jesus poses in the following passage.

2. Read Luke 6:46. Do you think Jesus' question here is addressed to just a few Christians or to many Christians? What makes you say that?

3. Think of people you know who call Jesus "Lord" but don't seem to do what He says. Why do you suppose they don't?

4. For you personally, what are some of the things that get in the way of obeying Jesus?

5. Read Luke 6:47-49. Here Jesus offers what He thinks is a compelling reason for obedience. He doesn't say, "Obey, or I'll punish you." What's His reason?

People who build houses without foundations (or with other building code violations) do it to save money. It costs less up front. They are betting that either (a) there will not be a flood, or (b) if there is a flood, the lack of a foundation won't matter. The logic of disobedience is similar: it costs less up front, and those stories about floods are just legends dreamed up by people who want to scare you.

6. What sorts of "floods" can flatten our "houses" when we're ignoring Jesus' instructions?

7. Is it really true that making a habit of obedience can help us survive the inevitable floods of life? If so, how does obedience help?

8. Think of someone you know who has made a habit of obeying Jesus, regardless of the up-front costs. How has that person's habit helped him or her survive a "flood"?

The Practical Benefits of Doing Things Jesus' Way

We sometimes think that doing things Jesus' way will bring us bondage, restriction, and unhappiness, along with a loss of personal choice. But just the opposite is true. I've discovered that saying yes to His will is the most freeing decision we can make. Here's why:

- *There is a hidden **power** in weakness.* Often we tire ourselves out trying to control everybody and everything around us. It takes an enormous amount of energy. However, the Bible says, "My grace is sufficient for you, for my power is made perfect in weakness" (2 Corinthians 12:9).
- *There is **freedom** in obedience.* When the Word of God is our guidebook, we don't have to live by a list of rules to establish "good conduct." Obediently following the principles outlined in the Bible brings the freedom to daily *choose* what is honorable, holy, and praiseworthy.
- *There is **fruitfulness** in doing things Jesus' way.* Jesus said, "If you remain in me and my words remain in you, ask whatever you wish, and it will be given you. . . . This is to my Father's glory, that you bear much fruit" (John 15:7-8).
- *There is **intimacy** in following His instructions.* The guideline is clear: "If you keep my commands, you'll remain intimately at home in my love" (John 15:10, MSG).

When we submit to God's authority, instead of being weak, we are strong. We find ourselves with an abundance of choices — and they all have the potential of bringing God glory and increasing our fruitfulness. But the greatest joy of all is experiencing His love intimately as we follow His commands, letting go of our control and discovering that obedience is actually "a glad surrender."

> *We need to let God be God, hour by hour, day by day, experience by experience, time after time. Our whisper, I love You, God, I trust You now . . . covers a great variety of things . . . And we lie there, praying that the Lord won't let us "waste" what is going on in any way.*
>
> —EDITH SCHAEFFER[2]

9. Think about these four benefits of obeying Jesus. Then think about a situation in your own life in which you are challenged to obey. Which of these four benefits is the hardest for you to believe—deep down in your gut—in this situation?

10. What encourages you to obey God in this situation?

Pair up with a partner. Tell your partner about an area of your life in which God is asking you to obey Him. Perhaps God is asking you to treat Him as a higher priority than something else. Maybe He's asking you to treat someone with love and respect. Take a couple of minutes to tell your partner how you'd like her to pray for you in this situation. Then listen to the area in which she'd like your prayer. You might write a few notes.

Gather again with your group. Begin your time of prayer by praising Jesus as Lord. What does it mean to you to call Him Lord? Then pray for your partner.

> *I discovered an astonishing truth: God is attracted to weakness. He can't resist those who humbly and honestly admit how desperately they need Him.*
>
> —JIM CYMBALA [3]

Ask God to show you more deeply at least one area of your life in which He desires you to obey Him more fully. Ask Him to show you a way to express your love and trust for Him through action. Ask Him to show you any area in which your effort to hold onto control is keeping you from loving God and others well. When you identify an obedience area, write it down.

Also, pray about your answer to question 9. Ask God to help you believe more deeply in the benefits of obedience.

Call or e-mail your partner (or if you're doing this study on your own, call a friend who will support your desire to grow in obedience). Give her an update on the area of obedience you're dealing with this week. Ask how her area of obedience is going and how you can pray for her.

3

PURSUE
COMPASSION OVER
CONVENIENCE

Compassion can never coexist with judgment because judgment creates the distance, the distinction, which prevent us from really being with each other. Often quite unconsciously we classify people as very good, good, neutral, bad, and very bad. These self-created limits prevent us from being available to people and shrivel up our compassion.

—HENRI NOUWEN[1]

WHEN my son announced he was marrying a divorced woman with two little girls, I balked at first. Then I *met* April. When I'd spent time with her, I realized why J. P. loved her so much. After hearing her remarkable testimony, I knew God had given me *exactly* the type of Christlike wife I had prayed my son would marry—

she just came in a different package than I was expecting. And it was April who taught *me* how to choose compassion over convenience.

A year after the wedding, my husband and I were visiting our children in Florida. We were driving downtown during rush hour. A man stood on the corner holding a sign: I'M HUNGRY. WILL WORK FOR FOOD. I heard April gasp. She knew what it was like for him because she once didn't have enough food for herself and her daughters — three-year-old Hannah and six-year-old Chelsea. I sensed her desire to do something for the man, but we were in the wrong lane, the light had turned green, and turning around would be inconvenient and time consuming. I thought of all the things we needed to accomplish that day and forgot about the hungry man on the corner. A few days later, my husband and I flew home to Michigan.

A week later April called. "Mom," she said, "Remember the man we saw on the corner — the one who was hungry? Yesterday I saw him again. I drove to McDonald's and they had a two-for-two-dollars special on quarter-pound hamburgers, so I bought one for me and one for the man on the corner, and I got Happy Meals for Chelsea and Hannah. But when we drove back, he was gone. We went down a side street, and we found him, but by that time he had two buddies with him and they looked hungry, too. I had two burgers in my hand — mine and the one I bought for the first man. And Chelsea and Hannah both had their Happy Meals in their laps. I asked if either of them would like to give up their burger to the third man. Hannah yelled, 'No way! I'm hungry!' But Chelsea took another look at the man and said she would give him her meal. Mom, I was so proud of her. Hannah's still young, but I'm sure she'll figure out when she gets a little older how good it feels to have compassion for others."

As I hung up the phone, I realized how much April was teaching me about compassion, too. In this session we'll see the importance Jesus placed on caring for the poor and suffering, and we'll examine some of the factors in our lives that interfere with a lifestyle of compassion.

1. When you were a child, what kinds of contact did you have with people poorer than you?

One of the great themes of the New Testament is that God offers us salvation from eternal death not on the basis of what we do, but solely by grace through the merits of Jesus Christ. All we have to do is put our faith in Jesus. This is solid gospel truth. Yet in the parable we're about to look at, Jesus uses some drastic language to describe how He expects His faithful followers to lead their lives. If we really believe in Jesus, how will we live?

Jesus tells the stories in Matthew 24–25 in response to His disciples' questions about the end times. They want to know when Jesus will usher in the end of the age (24:3), and Jesus gives them some signs to look for and a warning that no one will be able to pin down the date (24:36). Then He tells three parables to explain how His disciples should live as they await the end. The following story is the third of those parables.

2. Read Matthew 25:31-46. What's the setting for this story? When and where do the events take place?

3. On what basis does the King invite those on His right to inherit the kingdom (verses 34-40)?

4. On what basis does the King sentence those on His left to eternal fire (verses 41-45)?

5. What thoughts, questions, or feelings go through your mind when you read this?

6. Why do you think Jesus makes such a big deal about caring for the poor, the sick, and those in prison?

7. Read verses 35-36 again. Think about the following features of modern life. How does each feature make it harder to regularly do the things Jesus lists?

two adults in a family working full time to pay the bills:

living in the suburbs:

preoccupation with one's own material welfare:

the expectations of middle-class family life (keep a nice house, involve your kids in plenty of activities, and so on):

a feeling that the poor, the sick, the stranger, and those in prison are different from us:

other factors that come to your mind:

8. Do you do the things Jesus names in verses 35-36? If so, what trade-offs have you made in your life in order to have the time and money to do this? If not, what trade-offs do you think you would have to make in order to do these things?

9. To what level of involvement with the poor, the sick, strangers, and those in prison do you think God is calling you?

10. What one word best expresses the emotions you feel when you think about responding to this call? (For example, you might feel excited, scared, stubborn, content, guilty, convicted, joyful . . .)

> *What have you done today that only a Christian would have done?*
>
> —CORRIE TEN BOOM[2]

Understanding True Compassion
One of the great misconceptions about compassion is thinking of it as an *emotion* rather than an *action*. But compassion is

much more than feeling sorry for someone in need. True compassion is expressed when we *do* something about the need we observe. There are several practical ways we can become more compassionate:

- *Pray for **eyes** that see people's real needs.* Here's how Matthew described Jesus: "When he looked out over the crowds, his heart broke. So confused and aimless they were, like sheep with no shepherd" (Matthew 9:36, MSG). Pray that God will reveal to you people's physical and spiritual needs.
- *Develop **ears** that listen to people's heartaches.* One of the most powerful ways we can minister to people is to listen to them express their pain, hurt, and frustration. This means giving up the convenience of sticking to our preplanned agenda and making ourselves available to hear someone's need.
- *Engage your **hands and feet** in doing something constructive to help.* Instead of saying how sorry you are for someone's bad situation or unfortunate experience, list practical ways you can do something to "be Jesus" to that person. (For example, send an anonymous gift of money to someone in a crisis, baby-sit for a single parent, take groceries to a needy family, read a story to an invalid, go on a missions trip to a developing country, volunteer for a nonprofit organization like Prison Fellowship or Habitat for Humanity, keep extra non-perishable groceries in your car to give to homeless people, or spend a weekend caring for a mentally challenged child so the parents can have a "time out.")
- *Inspire others with your **heart** of love for people.* When we are engaged in acts of compassion, the joy of the giver is equal to or greater than the joy of the receiver. Motivate others to give up an evening or a day to get involved in hands-on compassion.

Compassion does have a price. It takes giving up some leisure time; sometimes it means getting our hands dirty; it can mean sacrificing a Caribbean cruise to spend our vacation on a mission compound. It always means responding to brokenness and doing something tangible to meet a need. Compassion is usually not convenient, but it's the most fulfilling way you can spend your life as a true Christ-follower!

11. Check the area you need to concentrate on over the next month:

☐ praying for compassionate eyes
☐ developing compassionate ears
☐ engaging compassionate hands and feet
☐ inspiring others with your compassionate heart

> *I see Jesus in every human being. I say to myself, this is hungry Jesus, I must feed him. This is sick Jesus; this one has leprosy or gangrene; I must wash him and tend to him. I serve because I love Jesus.*
>
> —MOTHER TERESA [3]

Pray for the hungry. Who in your city are hungry? Who ministers to them? Pray especially for women with children who are hungry. Pray for the sick and those who care for them. Pray for prisoners. Where is the nearest prison to your home? Pray for the families of prisoners. Does God want you to provide a gift of groceries or cash? Pray especially for women in prison, many of whom are nonviolent, drug-addicted mothers. Who are the strangers in your town: Immigrants? Refugees? Newcomers to your church? Pray for them.

Use Matthew 25:34-36 as a passage for meditation. Read it aloud to yourself. Listen to Jesus speaking to you. What phrase jumps out at you as a word from Christ? Chew on that phrase for a while. What is Christ saying to you here? How does your heart respond to these words? Take at least ten minutes meditating in this manner, then write down at least a few sentences of your response.

If you are already involved in a ministry of compassion, consider inviting another woman to join you. If you are not involved in such a ministry, talk with another woman who is. How does she make it work in her busy life? What motivates her? Make plans to join her once to see what her ministry is like.

> *Compassion is a sign of a truly great and generous heart. Compassion is understanding the troubles of others, coupled with an urgent desire to help. Man naturally is not compassionate. It is an attribute he must learn by living and by his own experiences. It is cultivating an ability to put [ourselves] in the [other person's] shoes, remembering that all facts and circumstances influencing the other [person] cannot be known to [us].*
>
> —MEGIDDO MESSAGE [4]

4

BUILD YOUR
FORGIVENESS
MUSCLE

Forgiveness is surrendering my right to hurt you for hurting me.

—ARCHIBALD HART[1]

ONE of my family members was in crisis, and some highly "character-damaging" information had become public. I found myself momentarily immobilized by my concern for the person I loved. I wondered how to take action that would be helpful but not too invasive, how to "be there" for the person who needed my support. My pain was deep, and several close family members and friends were feeling the difficulty of the situation, too.

Then the phone started ringing incessantly, and the mailman brought volumes of letters, all from people who had heard one woman's version of what took place. As I read the notes and took the calls, each person said, "You don't need to explain a thing.

Katherine (not her real name) gave us the details already and said your family really needed prayer."

As caller after caller named the same individual as their source, I knew my blood pressure was rising. I could physically *feel* anger brewing in my heart. Katherine had never even called to ask me if the information she was passing on to so many people was accurate, or if it had in any way become distorted by the time it reached her. She *assumed* it was true and took it upon herself to tell everyone she thought I had ever met the details as they had come to her. I felt even more disgusted that in the name of "a prayer request" she had passed on salacious information about someone I cared about deeply.

For days I nursed my hurt and fed my anger. Every time another phone call came or another letter named her as the contact person, I churned with a growing sense of internal hostility. My joy was gone; I was short-tempered with people; I was an agitated wife; and I withdrew from church activities. However, being this miserable with pent-up emotion takes a lot of energy, and my physical resources were already depleted.

One day my husband said, "Carol, have you begun to figure out that this situation is way out of our ability to control? We're proactive people and we like to 'fix' things, but we can't change what's happened. We also can't do anything to stop the Katherines in our lives. There are always going to be people who gossip about other people in the name of requesting prayer, but that's not our problem. When are you going to let go of your negative feelings toward this woman?"

Soon I was in tears. I had been allowing Katherine to control my life by giving her the power to immobilize me with anger and hatred. I was even considering how I could get back at her by telling others how insensitive she had been about her approach to the situation. The next day I picked up a magazine and cringed when I read the title of the lead article, "Forgiveness." The author said, "True forgiveness is never the result of human effort, but divine intervention. Confessing and receiving forgiveness for my own sin unleashed the power of the Holy Spirit within me. His love and supernatural presence brought about what I could not."[2]

That day I bowed my heart (and my stubborn will) and confessed my sin of anger toward Katherine. I prayed for God's forgiveness and asked Him to empower me to love her and to respond to my family crisis in a Christlike fashion. In this session we'll listen in on a conversation between Jesus and Peter about why forgiveness is so important, and we'll learn some things we can do to build our forgiveness muscle.

1. What is one thing for which God has forgiven you in the past month? You needn't share your most shameful secret. Here are a few possibilities to jog your mind:

- pride (thinking you are better or more important than others)
- envy (begrudging someone else's success, money, looks, or any other good fortune)
- greed (wanting more material possessions than you need)
- spiritual laziness (indifference about knowing God more deeply or growing spiritually)

- ingratitude (failure to thank God for the good things He provides for you)
- lukewarm love
- indifference to the poor

The point of question 1 is to become aware of how often God forgives us for serious sins, as well as for the same sin day after day after day. As we'll see in the following passage, our awareness of being forgiven is intimately tied to our readiness to forgive others.

2. Read Matthew 18:21-35. In Jewish thought, the number seven represented completion, perfection. What do you think is Jesus' point in verse 22?

3. To underscore His point, Jesus tells a story about the way things work in the kingdom where God is in charge. How is the servant contrasted with the king?

4. How does Jesus want us to respond to this story?

5. What do you think it means to forgive someone "from your heart" (verse 35)?

6. This story threatens a stiff penalty for unforgiveness. Why do you suppose this is such a big deal to God?

Many of us protest that it's unthinkable for us to forgive the person who hurt us most: the parent who abused us as a child, our ex-husband, or the friend who betrayed us. C. S. Lewis encourages us not to start with the heavy lifting but to build our forgiveness muscle gradually:

> *When you start mathematics, you do not begin with the calculus; you begin with simple addition. In the same way, if we really want (but it all depends on really wanting) to learn how to forgive, perhaps we had better start with something easier than the Gestapo. One might start with forgiving one's husband or wife, or parents or children, or the nearest N.C.O. [noncommissioned officer], for something they have done or said in the last week. That will probably keep us busy for the moment.*[3]

Also, forgiving others doesn't necessarily mean liking them, thinking they are good people, or saying that what they did was okay. After all, God forgives us while at the same time hating what we did and remaining committed to our becoming people who don't act like that. God envisions what we *can* be and *will* be when the Spirit is finished with us: like Himself. Forgiveness means letting go of the desire to punish people or see them suffer, and it means allowing ourselves to hope that someday, somehow they will become the humans they were meant to be.

7. What do you find challenging about forgiveness? Who do you find it hard to forgive, and why?

Building Our Forgiveness Muscle

It's easy to talk about the importance of forgiveness when no one has wronged you or when life is easy. However, when people rob you of your reputation, your self-esteem, your innocence, or your financial resources—or when they use their tongues, their resources, or their personal power to hurt someone close to you—it's easy to let your anger turn to bitterness. Here are some steps for building your forgiveness muscle:

- *Seek God's forgiveness for your own sins first.* It seems hardest for us to believe God will forgive us for our personal sins of the past. However, it is *never* too late to repent and receive God's grace. Have you committed a sin for which you have been afraid to request His forgiveness? Ask now and receive a new beginning.
- *Recognize that there are consequences for your past wrong choices.* We often assume "everything will be okay" once

we've asked for God's forgiveness, but we sometimes fail to realize that every action has consequences. That doesn't mean we haven't been forgiven.

- *Live above "the black cloud."* The apostle Paul writes, "Those who enter into Christ's being-here-for-us no longer have to live under a continuous, low-lying black cloud. A new power is in operation. The Spirit of life in Christ . . . has magnificently cleared the air, freeing you from a fated lifetime of brutal tyranny at the hands of sin and death" (Romans 8:1-2, MSG). The black cloud is condemnation for our sins.

- *Lavish the same forgiveness on others that God has so graciously given to you.* While Jesus was on the cross, men that He made were mocking Him. He lifted up on the nails in His feet (which caused excruciating pain) to get the breath to say: "Father, forgive them, for they do not know what they are doing" (Luke 23:34). If you are experiencing emotional pain because of the wrong choices of a parent, spouse, child, coworker, ministry partner, or anyone else, realize they may be responding out of dysfunction and hurt from their own past. Stretch your own arms out widely, bow your head, envision Jesus on the cross, paying for your sins, and say, "Lord, by Your power, I forgive those who have wronged me."

Don't be surprised if a *feeling* of forgiveness (either when you're forgiving yourself or someone else for past wrongs) doesn't flood over you. Your feelings will catch up to your action in time. Be content that God has forgiven you and you have forgiven others involved in your situation. Humanly speaking, none of us can forgive others the way we should, but with Jesus, it is possible. Keep flexing your forgiveness muscle!

8. Take a minute to think about whether there is any sin in your life for which you have not sought and accepted the

forgiveness God offers you. If you're meeting with a group, you may want to name the sin, but you don't have to.

9. What goes through your mind when you think about receiving God's forgiveness for your sin today?

> *If you are holding yourself captive because you can't forgive yourself for some past sin, God wants you to know that you can drop your sin into the river of His forgiveness and grace. . . . He wants you to leave the past behind and press on to a bright future.*
>
> —KATHY COLLARD MILLER[4]

Jesus taught us to pray, "Forgive us our sins, for we also forgive everyone who sins against us" (Luke 11:4). On a separate sheet of paper that no one else will see, take three or four minutes on your own to write the names of everyone you can think of whom you have not forgiven for something. Then fold this paper up and tuck it in your study guide for privacy.

During your prayer time, allow a space in which women can mention aloud the names of anyone they want especially to forgive today. It's not necessary to name everyone on your list, and you may want to follow C. S. Lewis's advice about not starting with the Gestapo. It would also be appropriate to confess any situations in which you are finding it hard to forgive. Ask God to forgive your inability to forgive. Perhaps that will help thaw the ice in your heart.

Lay before God the list of people you need to forgive. Jesus said, "Bless those who curse you, pray for those who mistreat you" (Luke 6:28). Pray for each person on your list. Ask God to give you a vision for who that person was born to be. Ask Him to deal kindly and mercifully with that person and to form that person in His image.

Share with someone your decision to build your forgiveness muscle and what you have learned from the experience so far. Be honest with her about any difficulties you have had in forgiving someone. (You don't have to give details of the offense.) Ask her if forgiveness is at all hard for her.

> *Forgiveness is the fragrance the violet sheds on the heel that has crushed it.*
>
> —MARK TWAIN[5]

5

ALLOW SUFFERING
TO PRODUCE HOPE

The longer I live, the more I begin to grasp that our
choice in life is never between pain and no pain. It is
rather a choice between enduring it and using it.
And God, in His great patience and love, gently
paves the way for its use.

—RUTH HARMS CALKIN[1]

THE call came in the middle of the night. A family member was in severe crisis. Someone close to me had been picked up by the police and accused of a serious crime. My husband took the call, and while he got the details, my body went into shock. I felt I couldn't breathe and fell on the floor with waves of nausea. Surely this event could not have happened. It was part of a cruel joke. Or perhaps it was just a nightmare and I would wake up in the morning to discover it had only taken place in my mind.

But morning came and the circumstances surrounding the

story were validated. Relatives and close friends needed to be noti-fied. Financial and legal arrangements had to be made. My mouth was so dry I wondered if my saliva glands had taken a vacation. I had to remind myself to take in air. My mind could contain only one thought at a time. Occasionally I heard my own voice say, *Just breathe and do the next thing.*

The next day I had a long-awaited appointment with my doctor for a routine checkup. As I entered the waiting room, full of women and children who were happily interacting with each other, I felt I was sitting on the edge of a scene I couldn't participate in. My mind swirled with strange thoughts: *How could these people be acting so* normal *when my whole life is falling apart? I wonder if they can see the pain on my face. I hope no one I know walks through that door because I just can't look them in the eyes. I guess God doesn't love me. I don't think I love Him either.*

When my name was called, I followed the nurse into an examining room. I hurriedly dressed in the lovely paper gown all women wear for their annual pap smear. When the nurse reappeared, I was sitting on the examining table and she said, "Are you okay?" At that moment I burst into tears. No, I was *not* okay, but it felt good to be near a compassionate person, even though she had no idea what prompted my emotion. She walked over to the table and put her hand on my shoulder as she said, "The exam won't be that painful."

It was the first time in twenty-four hours that I found myself smiling. I was surprised to hear myself laughing out loud. If she only knew what was happening in my life at that moment, she would have been surprised that I showed up for the appointment at all.

I felt betrayed, grief stricken, and hopeless. However, I'm dis-covering a better way to deal with pain in my life than "just coping." In this session we'll see how suffering produced hope for Jesus' mother, Mary, and consider how we can follow her example when we face suffering.

1. When you were a child of, say, ten or eleven years old, how did you deal with painful things that happened to you?

The apostle Paul writes,

> *We also rejoice in our sufferings, because we know that suffering produces perseverance; perseverance, character; and character, hope. And hope does not disappoint us, because God has poured out his love into our hearts by the Holy Spirit.* (Romans 5:3-5)

Unfortunately, the process Paul describes here is not inevitable. The vast majority of people don't rejoice in suffering, and their suffering does not produce perseverance, character, and hope. It often produces anger and either despair or numbness. Numbness refuses to hope for great things and instead watches television, reads romance novels, buys clothes, or eats chocolate to get through the week.

Suffering will do nothing for us unless we *choose* perseverance, character, and hope. To see how this works, let's look at

Mary, a pregnant teenager. An angel has told her that her baby is going to be the Savior of her people. She has embraced this calling from God even though it may mean the end of her engagement to Joseph and disgrace in her village. "I am the Lord's servant," she has told the angel (Luke 1:38).

To deal with this shocking news, Mary walks for several days to the home of her cousin Elizabeth, who is well past menopause but also pregnant.

2. Read Luke 1:39-56. Elizabeth's words in verse 45 are a good definition of hope. How does Elizabeth describe Mary's hope in that verse?

Gabriel Marcel defines hope as "a memory of the future."[2] That is, hope is being as convinced about what will happen (the future we envision) as we are about what has already happened (the past). Notice that in verses 46-55, Mary speaks in the past tense (God *has* performed mighty deeds) even though she is speaking of things God is going to do through her Son. She speaks about the future as though it has already happened.

3. What future events does Mary "remember" in verses 46-55?

Mary needs this firm memory of the future throughout her life. First, she has to face Joseph. Then after the baby is born, King Herod seeks to kill him, and Mary and Joseph have to flee to Egypt (Matthew 1:18–2:18).

4. Read Luke 8:19-21. Thirty years have passed. Jesus is gaining a reputation as a rabbi and wonder-worker. What suffering does Mary have to deal with now?

5. Put yourself in Mary's place. How do you think you would respond if your son treated you like this?

6. How would a "memory of the future" help you?

7. Read John 19:23-30. What suffering pierces Mary now?

8. What do you suppose keeps her from choosing despair or numbness now?

9. Even after Jesus is raised from the dead, ascends to the Father, and sends the Holy Spirit, the future she envisioned in Luke 1:46-55 still does not fully come to pass. The mighty men of Rome and Palestine still kill, tax, and persecute God's people. What do you think keeps Mary from becoming bitter or fatalistic as an old woman?

"Perseverance" can sound like digging in our heels and refusing to budge. But perseverance is not resignation. Nor is it holing up with a determination to survive. Mary never locks herself in her house. She never stops moving forward and taking risks. She is with the other disciples seeking God during the weeks before the Spirit descends on Pentecost (Acts 1:14).

10. What suffering still challenges you to persevere and hope?

11. What future do you need to remember?

12. What will the risk of moving forward look like for you?

Suffering Can Lead to Hope

Suffering is an integral part of life. During a recent seminar, I met a woman who had been paralyzed from the waist down in an automobile accident; a mother grieving over her daughter, who had been recently impregnated by her drug-addicted boyfriend; a wife watching her husband die from AIDS; a young couple whose baby had Down's syndrome; a single woman with breast cancer; a father who had lost his job due to corporate downsizing; and a young wife struggling with infertility.

Philip Yancey says there are three questions we ask when we are suffering, when we are questioning the goodness and trustworthiness of God: "When we ask our questions—Why is God unfair? Silent? Hidden?—we're really asking, Why is God unfair to *me?* Why does he seem silent *with me,* and hidden *from me?*"[3]

When you are in the middle of a painful experience, here are six specific action steps you can take:

- Write down a description of your trial.
- List anything that *didn't* happen in the your trial and verbally thank God for those specific blessings in prayer. (If you think hard enough, you can no doubt discover something else that could have made the situation worse than it was.)
- Ask yourself, "How did I contribute to the cause of this problem?" Write down anything that comes to mind. If there was a sin of omission or commission, confess that to God.
- Tabulate a new list of any benefits that might be developed out of this "season of suffering." (For example: compassion for others, a new ministry, personal and spiritual growth.)
- Meditate on God's character by writing out specific Bible verses that remind you of His goodness, justice, and mercy.
- Pray that God will bring a solution to the problem and that He will not waste this great sorrow in your life. Ask Him to teach you lessons that will deepen your compassion and enlarge your heart for others.

Each painful episode of suffering is an opportunity to meet the fiery darts of the Enemy with the shield of faith and a prayer that God's peace, which transcends our human understanding, will guard our hearts and minds as we choose faith over fear.

13. Think about the trial you mentioned in question 10. Choose one of the six action steps just listed, and take a

few minutes on your own to do that step. Write down your thoughts. Afterward, if you're meeting in a group, share with the group what you learned from doing this.

> *The dance of life finds its beginnings in grief. . . . Here a completely new way of living is revealed. It is the way in which pain can be embraced, not out of a desire to suffer, but in the knowledge that something new will be born in the pain.*
>
> —HENRI NOUWEN[4]

Pair up with a partner. Share with each other one situation that is calling you to choose perseverance and hope. It might be something that happened to you in the past that still hurts, or it might be a current episode of suffering.

Gather again with the whole group. Pray for your partner. Ask God to strengthen her to persevere. If you can, speak words that envision the glorious future God has in store for her. You can speak about God's heavenly kingdom or about the person your partner is going to become as suffering produces perseverance, character, and hope.

One reason we read the Bible is to remember the future. The Bible gives us glorious pictures of what's in store for us. We can look forward to being strong and tender women like Esther and Mary in this life, and we can look forward to the kingdom envisioned by the apostles and prophets.

Read Revelation 7:9-17 slowly. Read it again. Picture the scene in your mind. This is your future. How can remembering this future help you deal with what you face today?

Whom do you know who is suffering and could use some encouragement to persevere? First, pray for her. Then call or e-mail her. Allow yourself to really listen to what she's dealing with. Avoid giving advice ("You know, if you would just choose to persevere and believe God's promises . . . "). Instead, look for any sign of strength or character or hope you already see in her, and point that out. Share with her what *you* are believing *for* her.

> *A bird doesn't sing because he has an answer—he sings because he has a song.*
>
> —JOAN ANGLUND[5]

6

Cast Vision for the Next Generation

Vision is essential for survival. It is spawned by faith, sustained by hope, sparked by imagination, and strengthened by enthusiasm. . . . Vision encompasses vast vistas outside the realm of the predictable, the safe, the expected. No wonder we perish without it!

—Charles R. Swindoll [1]

Joyce Parks entered my life when I was a university student. She was the head of the public speaking department and soon became my academic advisor. I admired her enthusiasm for life and her ability to inspire students. When she walked on the campus grounds, there was energy in her step and a smile on her face. She exuded the kind of confidence I hoped to have one day.

I discovered that in addition to her professional commitment to the role of advisor, she also cared personally about developing my potential. Whenever I delivered a presentation in her public speaking class, she would write comments on my evaluation forms: "Your illustration really fit the point," or, "You are an outstanding communicator," or, "Good use of gestures," or, "You came across to your audience as a very approachable person."

Because she was my advisor, I had quarterly appointments with her. One day as I sat in her office, she put her pen down and said, "Carol, I think you have great potential for majoring in speech. I see qualities in you that would make a great teacher. You could also consider doing public speaking for Christian organizations and women's conferences. Your speeches are well prepared, but I also see a quality in your spiritual life that would fit very well with ministry. I'd love to coach you and encourage you as you follow through with where you see God leading you."

As I raced back to the dorm, my heart was singing and my mind was filled with creative ideas about what I could do with the rest of my life. Someone I respected had verbalized her evaluation of my abilities and voiced her expectations of what I could do with my God-given gifts. She painted a verbal vision of what I might be able to do for God's glory in the future. I knew my parents had confidence in me, but these comments that came from someone outside my own family were so affirming. I knew I had a mentor and a friend.

At one of our next appointments, Miss Parks handed me several books she thought would provide helpful research for my next few projects. She networked me with other Christian leaders and introduced me to people who could provide wise counsel regarding the career decision I would soon need to make.

Joyce Parks enabled me to experience what it feels like to have an older person "cast vision" for my future. She targeted me as a young woman with potential and took on the task of reinforcing my confidence and providing resources for the next step in my development. By modeling what it meant to cast vision for me, she taught me how to inspire other young women who would eventually look to me for wise counsel. In this session we'll watch Jesus as He laid out a vision for those who would carry on His mission after He was gone to heaven.

1. Name someone whose life or teaching has been an example you have sought to follow. (For the purpose of this discussion, choose someone who is not in the Bible.)

Mere hours before He was arrested, Jesus spent the evening equipping His disciples for what was to come. Had He been an ordinary revolutionary, He might have been mustering His forces and preparing them to fight. But Jesus was an extraordinary revolutionary, and He was preparing His followers for His death. Beyond His death would be His resurrection and ascension to the Father, but there would still be years (ultimately millennia)

of work on earth. His final vision casting session is described in John 13–17, but we will focus on chapter 17, in which Jesus laid out His vision as a prayer.

2. Read through John 17, and make a list of everything Jesus said He had done.

3. In what ways did these statements set an example for Jesus' followers?

4. Read John 17 a second time, listing everything Jesus asked the Father to do.

5. What does this list tell you about Jesus' vision for the next generation of believers? (What does it say about what He wanted them to be? To do?)

6. How do you think this prayer might have helped the apostles focus their own vision over the next several decades?

7. Has anyone ever helped you catch a vision of what your life is about? If so, how has that helped you? If not, do you think it would have helped, or do you think you've done fine without it?

Casting Vision for the Next Generation

The idea of "casting vision" may sound like an unusual phrase, but it's exactly what Jesus did for His disciples and what we can do for the women God leads us to mentor. It has to do with verbalizing the potential we see in younger Christian women and igniting their passion for living out the purpose God has for their lives. Here are some specific ways we can get started:

- *Think of a woman* who is younger than you are and who is in your current sphere of influence. Even if you are a young adult, there's a teenager who would love to know you better. (Perhaps it's your baby-sitter.)

- *Write down three positive descriptions* of the way she relates to people or uses her skills to benefit others.
- *Pray for her each day* and ask God to give you significant love and compassion for her.
- *Plan a time to meet with her.* This might be a formal appointment, or it might be a "mentoring moment" when you are spending time together because you are both involved in a ministry or a project at the same time.
- *Say something about the potential you see in her.* Brainstorm about ways she could use her gifts in a future career or ministry. Share your excitement about kingdom-building activities that match up with her interests and dreams.
- *Provide resources* (books, tapes, conference brochures, Bible study materials) that address her specific areas of interest.
- *Ask her these questions:*

    How can I help you?

    What are you passionate about?

    Would you like to get together to study the Bible?

    How can I pray for you?

- *If appropriate, engage her in a challenging, visionary task* that will make use of her spiritual gifts. Perhaps you can invite her to join you in a ministry project.

Becoming a visionary woman of influence is a risky, time-consuming, and costly choice. But there is no greater joy than investing your time in something that will last forever as you help younger women catch a vision of God's plans.

8. What do you think about this idea of casting a vision for the generation after you? What (if anything) do you believe

you have to offer? If your response is, "Not me!" what's behind that response?

9. How can you begin to cast vision for the generation after you? (Use the eight points listed on pages 69-70 for ideas.)

10. Of the six choices covered in this study, which one has hit home for you the most? How so?

> *Life becomes very meaningful and confident when we are sure we are walking in the direction God has given us.*
>
> —A. WETHERELL JOHNSON[2]

Use John 17 as a resource as you pray for the members of your group. You are finishing this study, perhaps taking a break or reaching a point of closure in your group. What vision has God given you for this group or individuals in the group? Speak that back to God in prayer.

If you have time, you can send each other off with something tangible to remember this session. Provide blank paper and pens for each woman. Write your name at the top of one sheet of paper and pass your sheet to the person on your right. Next, take a moment of silence to think about the woman whose sheet of paper you are now looking at. On this sheet, write one positive description of the way she relates to people or uses her skills to benefit others.

When you're finished, pass this sheet to your right. When your own sheet makes its way around the circle and back to you, you will have a written record of your group's vision for you. This exercise will work if you have only a few minutes to think, but it will be most effective if you give people a week's notice to think about what they'd like to write for each group member.

Vision is looking at life through the lens of God's eye.

—ANONYMOUS [3]

You can't pass on a vision if you don't have one. What is your life about? What is God doing through you? Take time to pray for clarity on these questions. (You might consider using *Six Steps to Clarify Your Calling* in this series.) Pray through John 17, and reflect on what God is saying to you through this passage.

WALKING WITH OTHERS

Even if you're only twenty years old and a new believer, you know some people in the generation after you. How can you pass on to one of those people the vision you have of God's agenda?

NOTES

Chapter 1: *Use Interruptions as God-Appointments*

1. Dr. Richard Halverson, quoted by Carol Kent, *Detours, Tow Trucks, and Angels in Disguise* (Colorado Springs, CO: NavPress, 1996), p. 17.

2. Marcel Proust, quoted by Linda McGinn, *Dancing in the Storm* (Grand Rapids, MI: Revell, 1999), p. 15.

3. Corrie ten Boom, quoted by Billy & Janice Hughey, *A Rainbow of Hope* (El Reno, OK: Rainbow Studies, Inc., 1994), p. 40.

Chapter 2: *Choose Obedience over Control*

1. Catherine Marshall, "The Joy of Obedience," quoted by Judith Couchman, *One Holy Passion* (Colorado Springs, CO: WaterBrook, 1998), p. 136.

2. Edith Schaeffer, *Afflictions* (Old Tappan, NJ: Revell, 1978), p. 115.

3. Jim Cymbala, *Fresh Wind, Fresh Fire* (Grand Rapids, MI: Zondervan, 1997), p. 19.

Chapter 3: *Pursue Compassion over Convenience*

1. Henri Nouwen, *The Way of the Heart*, quoted by the editors of *The Spiritual Formation Bible* (Grand Rapids, MI: Zondervan, 1999), p. 1329.

2. Corrie ten Boom, *Clippings from My Notebook* (Minneapolis, MN: World Wide, 1982), p. 115.

3. Mother Teresa, quoted by Billy & Janice Hughey, *A Rainbow of Hope* (El Reno, OK: Rainbow Studies, Inc., 1994), p. 45.

4. Megiddo Message, quoted by Lloyd Cory, *Quotable Quotations* (Wheaton, IL: Victor, 1985), p. 76.

Chapter 4: *Build Your Forgiveness Muscle*

1. Archibald Hart, quoted by Charles Swindoll, *The Tale of the Tardy Oxcart* (Nashville, TN: Word, 1998), p. 216.

2. Lorraine Pintus, "Forgiveness," *Virtue,* July/August 1997, p. 63.

3. C. S. Lewis, *Mere Christianity* (New York, NY: Simon and Schuster, 1996), p. 105.

4. Kathy Collard Miller, *Through His Eyes* (Colorado Springs, CO: NavPress, 1999), p. 153.

5. Mark Twain, quoted by Billy & Janice Hughey, *A Rainbow of Hope* (El Reno, OK: Rainbow Studies, Inc., 1994), p. 80.

Chapter 5: *Allow Suffering to Produce Hope*

1. Ruth Harms Calkin, *A Simple Gift, Gentle Reflections of God's Love* (Wheaton, IL: Tyndale, 1995), January 7 (from a perpetual calendar).

2. Gabriel Marcel, quoted in Dan Allender, *The Healing Path* (Colorado Springs, CO: WaterBrook, 1999), p. 78.

3. Philip Yancey, *Disappointment with God* (Grand Rapids, MI: Zondervan, 1988), p. 53.

4. Henri Nouwen, quoted by Linda McGinn, *Dancing in the Storm* (Grand Rapids, MI: Revell, 1999), p. 135.

5. Joan Anglund, quoted by Tim Hansel, *You Gotta Keep Dancin'* (Elgin, IL: David C. Cook, 1985), p. 113.

Chapter 6: *Cast Vision for the Next Generation*

1. Charles R. Swindoll, "Make Your Dream Come True," quoted by Charles R. Swindoll, *The Tale of the Tardy Oxcart* (Nashville, TN: Word, 1998), p. 606.

2. A. Wetherell Johnson, *Created for Commitment* (Wheaton, IL: Tyndale, 1982), p. 360.

3. Anonymous, quoted by Charles R. Swindoll, *The Tale of the Tardy Oxcart*, p. 607.

For information on scheduling Carol Kent or Karen Lee-Thorp as a speaker for your group, please contact Speak Up Speaker Services. You may call us toll free at (888) 870-7719, e-mail Speakupinc@aol.com, or visit our website at www.speakupspeakerservices.com.

THESE FIVE BOOKS REVEAL HOW YOU CAN MAKE A DIFFERENCE!

Six Basics of a Balanced Life

Learn to balance your life's priorities by settling your heart as Carol Kent and Karen Lee-Thorp show how Jesus is our most perfect time manager.

Six Essentials of Spiritual Authenticity

In an age in which public facades are the norm, the courage to be genuine is highly prized. Transform your life from acting like the person you want to be, to authentically living the life to which you are called.

Six Keys to Lasting Friendships

In today's busy world, the need for friendship is as strong as ever. Discover from Jesus how to build new relationships and strengthen the ones you already have.

Six Steps to Clarify Your Calling

Most people want to know that their lives count for something. Learn to make your life count as God's quiet voice leads you into the life He planned for you.

Six Secrets of a Confident Woman

Do you sometimes lack the confidence to make big decisions with relationships or take risks in career planning? Discover the courage and wisdom that come from replacing self-confidence with God-confidence.

Visit your local Christian bookstore, call NavPress at 1-800-366-7788, or log on to www.navpress.com.

To locate a Christian bookstore near you, call 1-800-991-7747.